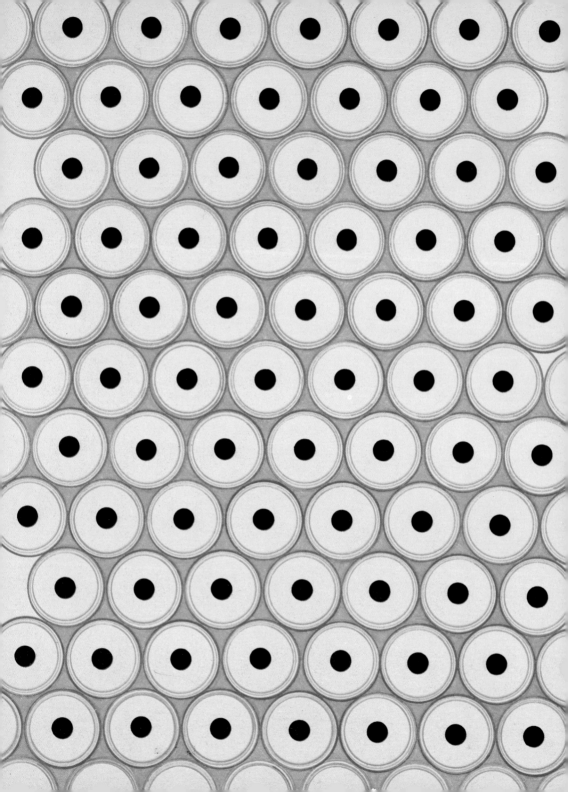

FROGS

designed and written by Althea
illustrated by Maureen Galvani

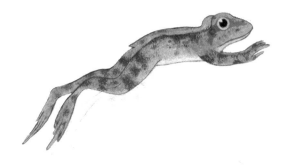

Longman Group USA Inc.

Published in the United States of America by Longman Group USA Inc.
© 1977, 1988 Althea Braithwaite

Originally published in Great Britain in a slightly altered form by Longman Group UK Limited

ISBN: 0-88462-188-X   (library bound)
ISBN: 0-88462-189-8   (paperback)

Printed in the United States of America

88 89 90 10 9 8 7 6 5 4 3 2 1

Library of Congress Cataloging-in-Publication Data

Althea.
  Frogs.
  (Life-cycle books / Althea)
  Summary: Describes the appearance, habits, and life cycle of this amphibian.
  1. Frogs--Juvenile literature. [1. Frogs] I. Galvani, Maureen, ill. II. Title. III.
Series: Althea. Life-cycle books.
QL668.E2A47 1988   597.8   88-13853
ISBN 0-88462-188-X
ISBN 0-88462-189-8 (pbk.)

Notes for parents and teachers
Life-Cycle Books have been specially written and designed as a simple, yet informative, series of factual nature books for young children.

The illustrations are bright and clear, and children can "read" the pictures while the story is read to them.

The text has been specially set in large type to make it easy for children to follow along or even to read for themselves.

It is spring at the pond.
A male and a female frog
are sitting on lily pads.
The male frog is croaking.

4

It is time for mating.
The female frog lays hundreds
of eggs in the water.
The male frog adds his sperm.

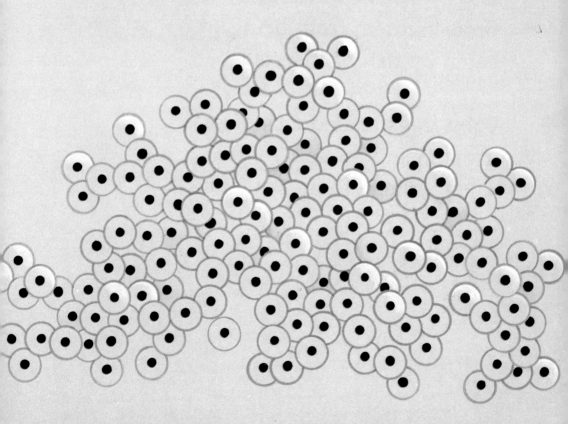

After the eggs are laid,
the frogs swim away
and do not come back.

The eggs are covered
with a soft jelly.
It keeps them warm and
protects them from being
eaten by fish or insects.

Baby frogs, called tadpoles,
grow inside the jelly.
They wriggle their way out.

Tadpoles look a lot
like small fish.
They have long tails
to help them swim.
They get air
from the water.

The little tadpoles
eat plants in the water.
They grow quickly.

After a few weeks
big changes begin.

The tadpoles still
live in the water
but their back legs
start to grow.

A few more weeks
go by and the tadpole
has front legs.
Other changes too
are happening inside
its body.

Now the tadpoles begin
to look more like frogs.
Their tails get shorter.
They swim up to the top
of the water to breathe
the air.

When their tails have
almost gone, the little frogs
climb out of the water
and hop away.

They are only as big
as a fingernail!

A frog uses its tongue
to catch moving insects.
It swallows them in a gulp.

Frogs eat a lot of food as
the summer goes by.
They get fat and
ready for winter.

The days are cool.
The frogs begin to hunt
for dark, damp places
to hide away.

The frogs rest through
the winter.
Their bodies get cold
but they do not freeze.

When it is spring
the frogs come out
of hiding and hunt
for food.

Three years go by and
the frogs are grown up.
They can lay eggs
to make more tadpoles.

FROGS are amphibians. They begin their lives in the water, behaving much like fish. As tadpoles, they have gills and take oxygen from water. Long tails are useful in swimming. But the tadpoles mature quickly, growing legs and absorbing their tails. They develop lungs and breathe air. Usually, however, they spend most of their lives close to water because their skins must not dry out. They are cold-blooded, that is, their body temperature depends upon their surroundings. In winter, if the climate is cold or dry, frogs hibernate, living off fat stored in their bodies.

Not all frogs are like those pictured here. Some are much larger; others have somewhat different life histories. The tree frog, for example, lives in trees and deposits its eggs in a frothlike nest hanging from a branch. Male frogs croak, make a clicking sound or chirp to locate females whose bodies are heavy with eggs. Mating for most frogs, with some exceptions, occurs as the female lays eggs in water and the male fertilizes them with his sperm. For most frogs, there is no guarding of eggs or young.

While thousands of eggs are laid, life is uncertain at best for the new generation. Fish, insects and birds eat frog eggs and tadpoles. Frogs are raised for human consumption, too.

Children are probably better acquainted with toy frogs, frog puppets and cartoon characters than with real frogs. But frogs are not just found in the wild and often can be heard calling on spring evenings near streams and ponds. They are not easy to see because their green bodies, often spotted, blend into their surroundings.

Because frogs have voracious appetites and consume insects of all kinds (and sometimes larger creatures like small snakes) they are welcomed—unlike their relative, the toads, which are often unfairly shunned. The destruction of marshes and rain forests and the pollution of ponds and streams, however, threaten both toads and frogs.

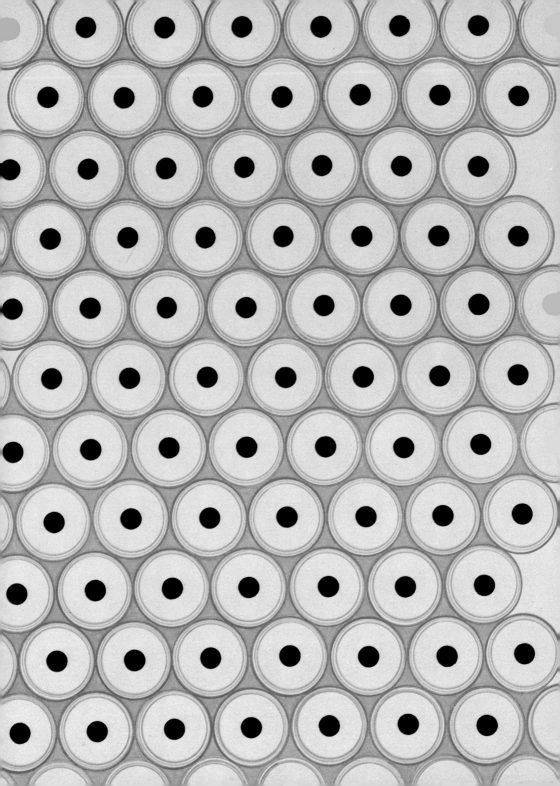

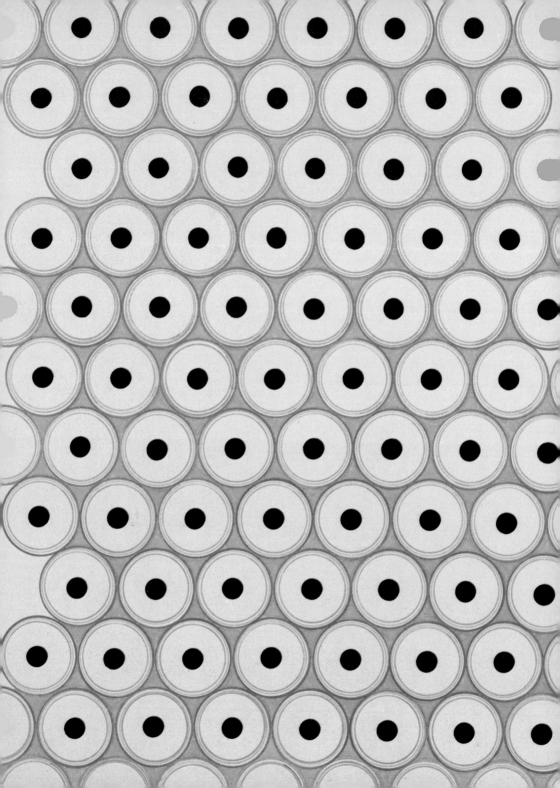